New Employee Orientation Guide:
90 New Employee Orientation Ideas for Human
Resources Professionals

Alisa Charles

New Employee Orientation Guide:
90 New Employee Orientation Ideas for Human
Resources Professionals
Copyright 2013 - 2017 by Alisa Charles

ISBN 10: 0989538516
ISBN 13: 978-0-9895385-1-0

About the Author

Alisa Charles is a certified Senior Professional in Human Resources (SPHR), (SHRM-SCP) with a Bachelor of Arts Degree in Communications from the University of Illinois at Chicago, and a Master's of Science Degree in Human Resources Management and Development from National Lewis University. She also holds a professional coaching certification from the Coaching and Positive Psychology (CaPP) Institute.

Alisa has worked for several large organizations in various human resources roles for over 20 years. In area, regional, and divisional HR leadership roles, she has had the pleasure of supporting the HR function for multiple locations across the country. This is where her passion for helping HR professionals began.

Alisa is also the creator of HRInventure, where she provides resources for **"inventive HR people with adventurous HR careers".** http://hrinventurenetwork.com

Alisa is married to Gregoire Charles and has three children; Marcas, Ashley, and Xavier.

Table of Contents

Introduction

You have probably heard of a phrase similar to, "You only get one chance to make a first impression." As human resources professionals, we know that this is also true about the first impression a company can make with a newly hired employee. From the time the employment offer is accepted, up to the first year of employment, there are so many opportunities in between to impress your new hire and make them feel a part of the team.

The objective is for a company to make a positive impression on their newly hired employee very early in the process. However, some orientation programs consists of simply having them arrive to work on their first day to spend two to three hours completing paperwork, watching a video, and receiving a two minute instruction on their job duties. Then they are left to figure out the rest on their own.

In a case like this, a new employee may feel that a positive orientation experience was not created for them. In fact, it would be almost certain that in this scenario, a new hire would not feel very welcomed to the company or motivated to become a part of the team.

As you think about your own orientation process, perhaps you feel that you have a pretty good program in place now, and you are simply looking for a few ideas to enhance your current program. Or maybe you are the HR leader within your organization and looking for a tool to share with your team on new employee orientation. Or you may have a process that is similar to my first example on orientation and looking for a change.

Whatever the case, the information contained in this guide will be helpful in developing the orientation program that will be the right fit for your company. Whether you are a part of a large organization or a small business, there are ideas you can use for your specific program. You will be able to take away several ideas to consider and to share with the other members on your team. You can then partner with your team to create a great experience for your newly hired employees.

My Thoughts on the Orientation Process

Very early in my career I was in charge of the orientation process at my office. The best way to describe my approach at that time was "I winged it". I was new to the company and for the most part was only aware of reviewing the handbook and providing the paperwork for new employees to sign. There was no real plan. Needless to say, I have been a part of many new hire orientations since then and have many ideas that I have picked up along the way to share with you.

I am sure you will agree that the orientation process is more than just a few hours of completing paperwork and watching a video or two on a person's first day. It's the opportunity to ensure that your newly hired employee starts off on the right foot with all the tools and information needed to be successful. Without a comprehensive process in place, you are at risk of not having a very satisfied or motivated new member on your team.

In general, a typical orientation program focuses on the company, including its history, goals, mission, values, and culture. It may also include some basic tasks such as completion of forms, payroll information, a tour, videos, and review of general policies and procedures. This is usually followed up by departmental information and training, and any additional training on internal systems, programs, products, and/or services.

However, the challenges that many HR professionals face with the orientation process can be summed up into five major areas:

1) The specific objectives of the orientation program have not been clearly defined.
2) The different needs of each individual new hire may not always be considered.
3) Lack of consideration that the process may cause anxiety or stress for some new hires.
4) The information being provided may not be delivered in the most effective manner.
5) A failure to ensure that new employees feel welcomed into the company.

With all the demands that exist in the workplace today, it

can be difficult to make the time needed to focus on this very important task. While most will agree that having a strong orientation program for new hires is important, it can often fall through the cracks, thus leaving the new hire, in some cases, to orientate themselves.

I am hopeful that the following information will provide you with some suggestions you can use to create or enhance your new employee orientation process by providing ideas that will:

- Generate excitement and make new employees feel good about their decision to join your company;
- Assist your new hire in learning the culture and values of your company quicker;
- Communicate expectations earlier in the process to ease anxiety and stress about starting with a new company; and
- Make your new hire feel as though they are already a valued member of the team.

To further assist you with your program, I have organized the following orientation ideas into several categories which should help you better determine which will be most useful for you. For example, I have provided ideas to help you *"Get Started"*. This is followed by ideas that are considered *"The Basics"*. These are ideas that are most likely a part of most orientation programs already.

There are some ideas that are a little more creative than your typical orientation program in a section I call *"Ideas that Rock"*. I have also included others that can transform your process by going *"Above and Beyond"* your typical orientation program.

Finally, I will share some parting thoughts for your consideration. After you have had a chance to review all the suggested ideas, you can go back to the section(s) that most closely fit the type of ideas you are looking for in your program.

Now let me warn you in advance that I will be sharing a lot of orientation ideas, thoughts, and suggestions which I recognize may seem a bit overwhelming. However, towards the end of this guide I will show you how to implement these ideas into a simple step-by-step plan that will assist you with incorporating them into your existing program.

Employee - Focused Orientation Process

As you review this orientation guide, there are some additional thoughts I want you to consider. During orientation, there is a lot of focus on getting new employees oriented to the company, its structure, process, and culture which are all very important. However, I would like to challenge you to also think about how best the company can become oriented to the new employee as well.

Your new employee was hired instead of other candidates most likely because of a strength or talent they possess that will contribute to your organization's overall success. The orientation process is a time where those abilities can be recognized, right at the beginning of their journey with your company.

According to an April 2013 article on Forbes.com, "*First Minutes are Critical in New Employee Orientation*", employee orientation programs are much more successful when the focus is centered more on the employee, and less on the company.

According to the research in the article, the study showed how by changing only one hour of the new hire orientation, to focus on individual strengths, it produced amazing results with a significant increase in retention and employee job satisfaction.

Some of the items that were added to one hour of the orientation process included the following:

- They conducted a fifteen minute discussion on how the company can enable new employees to express their individuality;
- They completed an exercise with new employees on their individual strengths. Each new hire shared how their strengths would be exhibited during a provided scenario; followed with a discussion on how their responses might differ from their fellow new hires;
- They each answered a series of questions about their individual strengths such as, *"What is unique about you that leads to your happiest times and best performance at work?"*
- They shared their strengths with their future co-workers; and

- At the end of the session, each new employee received a fleece sweatshirt embroidered with their individual names, along with a name badge; and were asked to wear them for the duration of employee orientation.*(As opposed to a shirt with just the company logo.)*

So, as you think about implementing the following orientation ideas, also think of ways you can balance the need for employee individualism and the need to orient them into the company culture.

Now let's get started! There is a lot of effort that goes into the recruitment process, from placing ads and conducting interviews, to coordinating a job offer. The following will focus on ensuring a strong and positive start for new employees.

New Employee Orientation Ideas
Getting Started

These first nine ideas will help you get started with working on your orientation process. By considering these ideas first, it will help determine how applicable some of the ideas that follow will be. Here are the first 9 ideas to consider for your program:

1. Review your existing process

As a starting point, I would suggest putting together a quick overview of your current process. You may already have this written in a formal document; or you may not have anything written at all.

Whichever applies to you, before you move forward with making changes or enhancements to your process, be sure you have all of the most current information on how new hires are being orientated at each level of the process.

The information you want is not just from an HR perspective, but from the other departments as well.

For example, you may want to check with your IT department and make sure you know the basics of how the computer set-up process works. Is there a form that a supervisor needs to complete? How much advance notice is needed?

You will want to learn the processes for all departments that are involved with new hires. To assist you with keeping track of everything, create a checklist with all of the applicable steps, and list the appointed persons for each area.

2. Listen and act on feedback from your employees

A very valuable piece of information that will assist you in taking your new employee orientation process to the next level, is to get feedback from your current and recent hires on their experience in joining your company.

This type of feedback is one way to learn what is working well, and what opportunities may exist in your process for improvement. Here are 3 ways you can obtain feedback:

- *Informal discussions* – you can simply ask recent new hires directly about how things are going, and what additional support could have been provided to assist in their transition into the company

- *Surveys* – a less direct approach could be in the form of a survey given to new hires. This can be an online survey, a paper-based survey, or a survey that is completed over the phone. Upon review of the results of your survey, you should have some information to assist you in determining some next steps with your process.

- *Exit Interview Data* – Another valuable tool that will help determine any gaps in your process is the data obtained from the exit interview, particularly if you are conducting an exit interview with employees who were relatively new to the company and decided to leave.

I remember getting feedback once from an employee who shared with me that she thought that all of the training she had to do was pretty overwhelming when she first started. She felt she was bombarded with training requirements she had to complete within her first few weeks on the job.

However, when the training was changed to be spread out over a longer period of time, feedback from another employee indicated that the pace was too slow.

Both of these forms of feedback were very valuable as it showed that the pace of the training will vary from person to person. So, incorporating options that allow people to go at their own pace would be a good way to address this feedback.

3. **Work group/orientation committee**

In thinking further about getting started with a review of your current program, consider starting a work team that includes a member from each department, and have them work together on developing a comprehensive orientation process.

If you are part of an organization that is spread out

over multiple locations, then a representative from each location could be a part of your work group. This way you can learn the best practices from the different locations and incorporate them into a company-wide program model which all of your locations can access.

The work group meets on a regular basis either in-person, via conference call (with or without video), or a combination of both. They will break out tasks and follow-up steps, keep the group updated on their progress during each meeting and provide a list of recommendations for consideration to the group lead/sponsor.

You will want to make sure that this work team has clear goals and that the expected deliverables from this team are clearly stated. It should also be communicated upfront what they can expect once their proposals have been submitted, including any review and/or approval process, and how the implementation of any new ideas would work.

What you want to avoid is having this team putting

in a lot of time and effort on this project, and then, when completed, it doesn't go anywhere, or there is no follow-up or communication with the team about next steps.

4. Planning meeting with orientation team

Coordinate a meeting with all those who participate in the new employee orientation process. This will help to clarify what everyone's role is in the implementation of the orientation program.

In fact, if you don't feel you need to start a work team as described previously, you could use this team as your informal workgroup. In your meeting you could ask for suggestions or feedback and incorporate any new ideas into your process.

5. Traditional or web-based program

If you are interested in incorporating additional technology into your new hire process, there may be features within your existing technology that you can consider. There are also several companies that offer software and online programs specifically for new employee orientation. Simply doing a search online will direct you to several companies available. Some of the features of these web-based programs include:

- The use of an avatar to show your new hire their virtual path within each phase of their new hire process;
- Resources and information made available to them online, based on where they are in the new hire process; and
- Social networking tools to chat with other new hires, connect with mentors, create a personal network, or interact with senior leaders and departments.

So whether you use a traditional process, a web-based process, or a combination of both, knowing what method you will be using ahead of time will better determine which of the following suggestions will be most applicable for your orientation program.

For example, there are some suggestions I will discuss as an individual idea but if you use a web-based process, some of the suggestions may already be included into your web-based program.

If this is the case, then you can also take the opportunity to review your set-up within your web-based program to determine if it has the most current information, and revise it as appropriate.

6. **New hire website**

A new hire website is another option that may already exist within your current technology via a company intranet structure already in place; or it may be part of a larger online program. By having a new hire website, many of the resources can be provided to your new hire by sending them a link to the site. Here they have access to paperwork, company information, pictures, etc. This is a great opportunity to start the transition process sooner by providing the link early in the process.

7. **Pre-Boarding/Onboarding process**

In general, pre-boarding is the process between when the offer is accepted and the employee arriving on their first day; and onboarding is on or around the first day on the job, and up through the first year of employment. This is the best opportunity to help your new hire learn and understand the company quickly and without the stress of having to figure out the in's and out's of your company on their own. During the pre-boarding, you can provide:

- Company information (i.e., mission, values, newsletters);
- Benefit information;
- New hire paperwork;
- Orientation schedule of activities; agenda;
- A sponsor or mentor to answer any questions they may have before the first day; and
- Networking opportunities to meet employees before their first day (i.e., informal gathering with peer employees, provide pictures of the team where it makes sense, etc.)

The purpose of providing this earlier is to help to better prepare them for the first day/week on the job. Also, if there are regularly scheduled meetings, conference calls, or other activities of which they need to be aware of, this can be provided in advance so they are better prepared. Other items that could be shared during this process is information on dress code so they are aware of what is considered appropriate attire, and the layout of the office, etc. These steps can be helpful in setting up the first day to be as smooth and stress-free as possible for your new hire.

I will be providing more details and various options to assist you with accomplishing these objectives throughout this guide.

8.   Orientation locations

Be creative with where to hold your orientation meetings. For example, you may want to start off in the conference room. However, to make it more hands- on and interesting, you may want to move a portion of the meeting into a different area.

This could be at a location outside of your building, or it could be in a department, or a location they will be working in.

9. Budget

Determine what type of budget (if any) that you will have to work with for your new employee orientation program. This will be helpful in determining which ideas will keep you within the budget.

The Basics

If I could sum up my philosophy on what makes up an effective new hire orientation program in 3 steps, here is what they would be:

Step 1: Ensure that your new employee feels welcomed to your company from the moment they decide to accept the offer of employment;

Step 2: Provide a well-planned first day, first week, and ongoing for up to the first year of employment;

Step 3: Ensure a follow-up process where all needs are met in a timely manner.

The following ideas are designed to cover some of the basics of what is generally included in an orientation program. For some this may be a good starting point if you do not have a formal program in place at the moment. For others, this may be a great place to review against your current program and consider additions or enhancements to your program to ensure all the basics are covered.

These are not listed in any particular order, so you can pick and choose ideas that will best fill a gap and/or enhance a piece of your current program. You can also determine where these ideas will fit best: for example, some could be put on a website, a new hire folder, a flyer, or placed on a bulletin board dedicated to new hires. Determine what is most appropriate for your company.

10. A welcome message

Soon after an offer of employment has been accepted, you can send out a welcome greeting via email or you could send a letter in the mail. You could even send a card with all of their new team's signatures and a welcome message.

A welcome message can be very simple with colorful fonts, pictures, and graphics that read something like "Welcome to the Team!!" Or, "We are looking forward to you joining the team." You can also advise them on the next steps, such as when they can expect the offer letter, and any additional instructions such as drug screen, background check, etc.

This step could also be completed at the time of

sending out the offer letter. This step should be particularly well organized as the offer letter may come from a different source (i.e., recruiter, supervisor, other). You will want to ensure that a welcome message is not sent out before the offer has been officially extended or accepted.

11. **Welcome phone call**

Between the time an offer of employment is accepted, to the first day of employment, a manager, future peer, or mentor can be designated to give the new hire a phone call to once again welcome them to company. They can also offer to answer any questions the new employee may have.

This is also a good time to reiterate any information the new hire will need regarding their first day such as where to park, which door to enter, or if there are any special instructions when entering your facility.

Finally, the company contact can provide the new employee with their contact information as an additional resource for any questions they may have later.

12. Prepare for your new hire

Here are 3 tips that will ensure that your newly hired employee has a strong start in their new role by preparing for their arrival.

1. Set a clear plan in advance;
2. Ensure all participants in the orientation process are clear on their role; and
3. Follow through with the plan.

Perhaps one of the biggest reasons that people fail in their new position is the lack of tools needed to be successful. Therefore, you will want to prepare for your new hire and ensure that all of the tools and resources are provided in a timely manner.

The last thing you want is for your new hire to show up to work and their work space is not ready, or their computer is not set-up, or they have no access to anything they need to get started. If you do not have one already, you should create a **"New Hire**

Checklist" that organizes all the steps that need to happen prior to your new hire's arrival. This could include ordering business cards, note pads, office supplies, uniforms, time cards, security badges, and whatever is applicable for your company.

There are other types of checklists that you can develop separately, or as one comprehensive checklist which includes the following:

- Before the First Day checklist;
- Tour Guide checklist;
- The First Day checklist;
- The First Week checklist; and
- 30-60-90 Day Follow-Up checklist.

These checklist items are designed to help keep the process on track and ensure all of the steps are covered.

13. Computer access, email accounts, passwords, etc.

By partnering with your IT department and department manager, you can ensure that your new hire receives timely access to their computer, email accounts, etc.

14. Laptops, cell phones, etc.

If your new team member will need a laptop or cell phone, again you can partner with your IT department or office management to ensure that these items are delivered in a timely manner.

The new hire should also be provided with the information needed on how to obtain assistance with their equipment if it is needed.

15. Business cards and office equipment

If you are able to, order business cards and any other type of office supplies that may be needed in advance. This way, these items can be made available to your newly hired employee on their first day.

It will be nice for them to walk in to their new space and see that these items have already been ordered and displayed at their workspace and ready for them to use.

16. Badges, name tags, uniforms

Instructions on how to obtain their security badges, name tags, or uniforms should also be communicated to your new hire.

Anything that can be ordered prior to their arrival on the first day should be done. Having these items available on their first day, or soon thereafter, will assist that new team member in transitioning into their role more quickly.

17. Introduction to the team

Make sure, managers and employees are available to meet the new employee and greet them as soon as possible. Everyone should have advance notice that there is a new employee starting so that they can be aware and have a planned interaction with that person.

In some organizations, there may be opportunities for your new employee to interact with their teammates before they even start. As mentioned earlier, this could involve social networking sites for new employees, or other opportunities within the team such as informal social events.

18. New hire lunch

Have a planned lunch. This could be a one-on-one lunch with the supervisor at a nearby restaurant. Or, if your company has a meal service there, they can prepare something special.

19. Tour

Getting your newly hired employees familiar with their work environment is important and can be accomplished by conducting a tour.

Ensure that there is time scheduled so that someone is facilitating this important task. This is where they are shown everything from where the time clock is located, to important entrances and exits.

Other important areas that should be included are: work area, fax machine, copy machine, restrooms, conference rooms, supply room, vending machine, and staff parking.

20. Telephone procedures

Here you can include any special instructions on accessing the phone system. If a password or special code is needed to access the system, it is best to let your new hire know this immediately.

Also, provide them immediate access and instructions to set-up their voicemail, instruct them which numbers are pre- programmed, and provide a tutorial on how to transfer calls or use the conference call line feature.

Again, I recognize that this may fall under someone else's responsibility, such as an office manager. In any case, you will want to know when this occurs in the new hire process, and exactly who is responsible.

21. Security and security codes

Security is an important issue today in ensuring the company and its employees remain safe. When appropriate, be sure to share access information as needed.

This could mean access to the front door to enter building, to workspace areas, etc. You want to avoid having your new hire wait around for access to things, areas, or spaces that they need to access in order to learn their job. Anything less could be quite frustrating to your new employee.

Also, if certain identification is required or signature needed for access, make sure your new employee is well informed and prepared so they know what to expect and will not be surprised.

22. Orientation presentation

Most presentations are in a PowerPoint format. There are many things you can include in your presentation to keep it upbeat and engaging such as: colorful fonts, graphics, and anything to make it interactive such as questions where viewers are asked to provide answers. You can also include pictures of people such as your executive team, department members, and pictures of recent employee events.

You want to avoid reading directly from the slides and use them more as a guide to have a more conversational meeting instead of providing tons of information with limited opportunity for the new hire to interact.

23. Orientation speakers

Having other people present during orientation gives your program a little variety for your new employees and keeps the orientation interesting.

In order for your speakers who perform presentations during your orientation meeting to be effective, they should present only the essential information. Also, there should be use of good presentation skills and techniques, and professional looking visual aids.

24. Company mission, culture and values

Here is your opportunity to let your organization shine by providing all sorts of information about the company. Generally, you start with your company's mission, vision, and values.

Additionally, you can include the history of your company, company profile, sales information, and success stories, etc.

25. Workplace videos

Depending on your company and/or type of business, the list of videos that are typically shown during an orientation meeting will vary. Some of the basic types of videos may include a company welcome video, training on various topics such as harassment, drug-free workplace, fire safety, workplace safety, and employee benefits.

You may have the option for including some of these videos online where your new hire can view them at their convenience.

26. Paperwork & new hire packet

In my view, I feel that HR departments have a bad reputation of being all about the paperwork. But today, much can be done electronically. Determine what forms can be sent to your new hires electronically in advance. This will certainly reduce the amount of time they are spending completing forms, and focus more on engaging them with others, meeting and talking with their new co-workers, peers, etc.

For those forms that must be completed in person, you should present them in a nice employee packet. You could use a customized folder, label, or envelope with the company logo, and the new employee's name. Make sure you use nice clean copies of the paperwork, and avoid using a copy of a copy.

27. Employee handbook

In some cases, your employee handbook can be distributed to your newly hired employee prior to their first day on the job. Some include the handbook with the offer letter that is sent out.

Whether this is provided in advance, or during the orientation meeting on their first day/week, be sure that you dedicate time to go over the expectations that are listed in the handbook.

While there is no expectation that you will read every word of the handbook during your orientation meeting, you will want to go through the main points. (In the next section I will share some ideas on how you can turn this into a fun exercise.)

28. Job description

Provide your new employees with the job description for the positions in which they have just been hired. This should be reviewed with them during the orientation if the meeting includes others who have been hired for the same position.

If the orientation includes new employees from a variety of positions, then their specific job description can be reviewed with their supervisor during the department specific orientation.

29. Policies and procedures

If you have policies or procedures that need to be reviewed in addition to the handbook, you can print out the applicable information and include it with your new hire packet.

In most cases, your policies or procedures will include greater detail than what you have written in your handbook. As result, where appropriate, include some of your policies for review with your new hires during the orientation process.

30. Payroll

Include communication and training on your payroll process as appropriate. Have available a payroll schedule that shows the payroll cycle, pay periods, and pay dates. Federal and state tax forms (where applicable) should also be provided.

Provide information on electronic pay options such as direct deposit or debit cards where their pay can be directly deposited into a bank account or special debit card on each pay date.

You may also want to consider partnering with a few financial institutions in your area that may be willing to work with you to offer your employees special accounts or programs. If so, you could include their brochures or information for employees to contact directly.

Where applicable, review the expectations regarding overtime, recording hours worked, time off practices, and how they all impact the paycheck.

31. Business hours

Many companies today operate their business during various times up to and including 24 hour operations. Therefore, it is important to communicate the hours, or shifts, your new employee would be expected to work.

Whether it's Monday through Friday, weekends, or evenings, it is important that the expectation of the days and times they are expected to work are clearly communicated. This way your new employee is aware of the expectations before they start.

There is nothing like a new hire believing that they have a Monday through Friday position, only to be told after they start that the expectation is that they work some weekends and/or evenings. There are several work/life factors that play into someone's schedule such as schooling, daycare, and other commitments, so ensuring that everyone is on the same page at the very beginning will avoid confusion and frustration later.

Also, if your organization offers a flexible schedule or flex-time, here is a great opportunity to communicate this as well. There may be a policy to review or a form they can complete where they can

select a set flexible schedule right at the beginning
of their employment.

32. Dress code

I mentioned this briefly under "#4 Pre-
Boarding/Onboarding". Providing information
about your company's dress code is important so
that your new hire is clear on the attire. For
example, if they start on a Friday when your
company observes casual Fridays, you wouldn't
want them showing up to work in a suit.

Different organizations have different expectations
regarding what is considered appropriate attire.
Consider that your new employee may be coming
from a company with different expectations on
dress code. This will help you to clarify what is
acceptable attire for your organization. This will
also help to avoid any awkward moments or
conversations with your new hire down the road.

33. Organizational chart

Share your company's organizational structure with your new employee. This can be accomplished by sharing your company's organizational chart. This should be reviewed with your newly hired employee so they can learn how they fit into the organization.

By sharing this information, they get a better idea of your organization's structure and can more quickly become familiar with how information flows within your organization.

A discussion of the employee's department's function, goals, and its relationship with other departments should also be included. Also include the sharing of roles and responsibilities of other department members as appropriate.

34. Benefits and health & wellness information

For those new hires that are benefit eligible, your orientation packet is another great place to put any additional information you may have regarding benefits.

Your benefit provider may have additional communication such as flyers with important telephone numbers, or services that they offer. With the rising costs of healthcare, you can provide information on any health and wellness initiatives that may be going on at your company as well.

35. State or industry specific requirements

Each state and industry have different requirements so you will want to make sure your process incorporates any specific requirements that apply to your company.

36. Workplace Safety

Be sure to clearly communicate your company's position on workplace safety. If you have a safety program in place, include the details of the program during the orientation process. You can also include safety tips and instructions on who to contact if they see any potential hazard.

Ideas That Rock

This next section includes 33 additional ideas for you to consider that are a little more creative than those you found under the basic ideas. There are some ideas listed in this section that were discussed previously, however the concept is expanded here to include a much bigger idea.

37. New Employee Personal Profile

You could request in advance that your new employee completes a profile that shares some fun facts about them; things such as favorite movie, color, TV show, sports, hobbies, etc. By getting to know more about your new hire in advance, you can plan little surprises in the orientation process that relate to something of interest.

This could be completed as an online profile where applicable, or it can be a paper-based questionnaire.

38. Welcome letter from the President

As a company, you could decide that a letter will be

sent to all new employees from the President, or another member of the Executive Team.

A letter like this will send a strong message that new employees are valued even at the highest level of the organization.

39. Welcome gift/gift basket

Why not welcome your new hire with a special gift? This could be an item with the company logo such as a shirt, or a bag. You could also consider things like office supplies, candy, flowers, or other treats in the form of a gift bag. You could even pull information off of their personal profile and purchase a welcome gift related to something they like. For example, if a hobby is listed as "enjoys planting flowers" purchase a book on flowers, or flower seeds that can be planted, etc.

I remember at one of my companies, I selected a really nice gift box of various treats to give out to new employees during orientation. It came in a decorative box that had royal blue wrapping with beautiful gold ribbon tied around it. It looked so classy that I was always excited to present it to the new employees when they went through orientation.

It was great for each new employee to set their fancy gift box on their desk for others to stop by, share a treat, and engage in conversation with employees who stopped by to greet them.

40. Post a picture of your new hire

Prior to their arrival you could have them send you their favorite picture electronically. Then you can print and post it in an area visible to both your new hire and employees. Your new hire would be able to tell that their arrival was anticipated. It also gives your current employees an awareness of who is starting, and how they can further assist in the welcome process.

41. Welcome stand near entrance with new hire information

Imagine entering your company's reception area

and right there, next to the receptionist is a stand that reads "Welcome Your Name" for all visitors and employees to see. Imagine how welcome your new employee will feel.

This happened to me in one of my first HR jobs. I remember my name being posted there right in the front of the reception area. I felt very welcomed by that and I saw that it was done for every new hire after me as long as I was employed there.

That was many years ago, so the fact that I still talk about it today shows how much of a positive impression it left on me.

42. Newsletter

Create a newsletter that introduces the new employee to the team, department, and company. This could include a picture, fun facts, and announcements.

Or if you have an existing newsletter, dedicate a section just for new employee information.

43. New hire buddy/mentor

Assign someone to be a buddy or mentor for the first few weeks of employment. This will usually be a peer that can assist with general questions during their transition process. By having a point person (other than their boss) they quickly get to blend in with the team.

This should be someone who has had a positive history with the company and can be introduced to your new hire early in the process.

As discussed in previous sections, the earlier in the process you can make that connection with the new hire, the better your newly hired employee's chance of a smooth transition into your organization.

44. Games

What can I say, I love games. I guess some would say that I can be a bit competitive at times when it comes to games. If you would like to add a little fun to your orientation program, here are 6 types of games or activities you can consider:

- **Ice Breakers** – Here is where you could play an activity to help your new hires get to know each other a little better. In addition to their name and new position, ask them to share a fun fact or information about themselves where one item is false. See if the other new hires can figure out which fact is false. You could also search online for ice breaker activities that will help your new employees relax, have fun, and expedite the process of getting to know each other.

- **Fun Facts Guessing Game** – In this game, your new hires write four fun facts about themselves on a note card and place in a basket or box. One at a time, they would each pick up a notecard and read the information, trying to guess which person it belongs to.

- **Quiz** - Create a quiz that can be taken at the beginning and/or end of their orientation (pre-test/post-test). Have prizes for those with high scores, or offer a prize to everyone for their efforts.

- **Fun Forms** - Other options to assist with retaining the information that they have learned in a fun way are things like crossword puzzles, word matching games, or fill-in-the blank forms. Create these forms and have a race to see who completes it first, giving prizes here as well.

- **Matching Game** – Once your new employees have had the opportunity to be introduced to the team or department, have a picture of each employee on the team and have them match the pictures of the employees with their name.

- **Find and Sign** – This game requires that a list be provided to your new employees with names of other employees for them to locate. Once they locate them, they introduce themselves and start building that relationship right away with a few minutes of conversation. Then they obtain the signature from that person on the list that is provided.

- **T.V. Game Show** –Create a game board with different categories and dollar or point values. The categories would be the different areas covered during orientation such as the handbook, benefits, mission and values, or fun facts. Develop questions for each category in advance. Divide the group into teams and select a facilitator. Have the teams take turns answering applicable questions. When a question is answered correctly, the team is awarded the dollar amount or points. When answered incorrectly, the other team is given a chance to answer the question. Continue the process until all participants play a few rounds, and then award prizes to the winning team.

45. Raffle

This idea is particularly fun if you have a large group of new hires all at the same time. You could issue raffle tickets or simply put their names in a box and raffle off different prizes such as company merchandise, free meal, gift basket, etc. You could also make a game of it. For example, every time you ask a question about the company, their job, etc. when they get it right, their name goes into the raffle for multiple chances to win a prize.

46. Scavenger hunt

There are several options to consider with regard to a scavenger hunt. One approach is a format that will assist your new hire in learning the information that is being covered during the orientation meeting, such as the review of the company handbook. Rather than review each section, you could turn the review into a game.

Divide the group into teams of employees and give them a list of questions to answer, using the handbook for example. Choose questions about important information that your new employees need to know. They look through the information you have already provided to find the answers.

Have a real scavenger hunt throughout your company where your new hires have to locate certain people, places, or things throughout the building. Leave a note or clue at each landmark, or have them take a picture at each landmark they locate.

To make it exciting, turn this into a race in either scenario where they would have to complete questions or tasks within a certain timeframe. Have prizes for the winners and/or for everyone for their participation.

47. New employee reception

This is an idea where the new hire lunch discussed under the basics section is expanded to include the department, the team, etc. Everyone would be invited and can meet and greet your newest team member.

This could include a light snack or meal for all attendees. You could also incorporate a small program as part of the reception if desired.

48. Brown bag lunch with all new hires

Another variety to the new hire lunch is the brown bag lunch idea. At the beginning of your new hire's employment schedule a brown bag lunch event where they bring their own lunch (or lunch can be provided) and are invited to eat lunch with the President, departmental heads(s), etc. This would be an informal time where there is no formal agenda, but just a time to eat and get to know a member of the management team better.

49. Complimentary meal or treat

Create a special coupon for new employees for use during their first month on the job which entitles them to eat for free in the eatery inside your workplace or building.

Or you could partner with some of the local restaurants in your area for a complimentary meal or treat. Or simply purchase gift cards to a nearby eatery and offer them to your new hire to get a complimentary meal or treat that could also be used within their first month.

50. All employee meeting recognition

If you have employee meetings on a regular basis, have an item on that agenda to welcome your new employee. You can introduce them with some fun facts and information on what they will be doing for the company. You could also have them say a few words.

51. Welcome book or picture

Have a book or picture that the team members all signs with welcome messages. Then present that to your new employee. If someone is coming from a different city, you could purchase a book about your city, have everyone sign it and present it to them.

52. List/Brochures of nearby locations

Have a list handy to put in your new hire packet that lists nearby places they can go for lunch and other personal business like cleaners and currency exchange.

This is especially helpful for those working in your location for the first time. Although there are many website and apps that can show your new employee where to go for certain things on their own, providing this information is a small gesture that can go a long way in showing consideration for your new team member.

53. Transportation information

Provide information on transportation such as bus or train schedules. Also include important telephone numbers such as local cab companies, parking information, etc.

54. Parking spot

Imagine being a new employee and being told that there is a dedicated parking spot right in front of the workplace, with your name on it and it is available for your first week of employment? How would that make you feel? This is a great gesture to show your new employee that they are important and you are glad they are there.

55. Health & wellness activities

Hire a health and wellness expert to be part of your orientation program. For example, bring in a yoga expert who could go over some chair yoga exercises for 30 minutes, particularly if your business is an office environment where there is a lot of sitting.

The fitness expert could go over techniques that employees can do right in their chair throughout the day to help them stay healthy and injury free. They could also go over other techniques that would assist those who do a lot of standing on the job.

Other ideas could be inviting a fitness expert to come and talk about food, nutrition, and diet. Even a massage therapist to provide a little stress relief by making a professional massage available to your new employee would be welcomed.

56. Benefit orientation for family members

Consider holding part of the orientation meeting in the evening so that the new employee's family can attend as appropriate. This way they are able to participate in the selection of the health plan that is right for their family, as well as get information first hand.

If an in-person meeting is not feasible, then access to recorded information on enrollment options or processes would be effective also.

57. Perks and discounts

Who doesn't like free or discounted products or services? Research free or discounted services and include in a flyer in your packet. Check with some of your vendors and see if they are willing to offer discounted services to your employees. This information can also be included in your packet.

58. Department rotation

Most employee orientation programs are good at giving a tour of the department, facility, office, etc. Go a step further and have the new hire spend some time in each department. This will help them see the big picture and help them put into perspective how what they do will fit into the bigger picture.

59. Links to tools and resources

Provide a page or email that has helpful links and resources right at their fingertips. Whether it is short cut to access company information, or links where they can order food, drop off dry cleaning, order photos, or whatever you think would be useful.

60. Donate for a cause

If there are specific company sponsored charities that your organization partners with, include information on this as part of your orientation program. This could include a presentation from employees who participated in the last event, or pictures or videos about the charity, events, etc. This information may inspire your new employees to want to donate a portion of their earnings for a cause.

61. Volunteer opportunities

There are many volunteer opportunities for organizations that wish to participate. If this is something that your company participates in, then the orientation program is not only a great place to share with them your company's involvement, but you could also invite them to participate in any future events.

62. Information on company activities

Does your company have a sport team, or Toastmaster's club? Have members on the agenda to talk about the club or team and how they can participate if they choose.

63. Complimentary uniform, tools, materials

Consider including a complimentary item from your business. This could range from a complimentary uniform item, tools or materials.

Offer a nice presentation of these items in a gift bag, or put them all in one big bag and pass it around for each new hire to randomly pick an item to keep.

64. Company merchandise

Consider giving away company merchandise such as a company shirt, jacket, or hat. If your company sells a particular item or service, you can present that to them during the orientation process.

Receiving a gift can be a lot of fun. It is also an excellent way to reinforce to your newly hired employees that they are welcome.

65. Employee recognition opportunities

If you have a recognition program at your company, create a flyer with the specifics to include in your orientation program. This could be your "Employee of the Month" or "Years of Service Award" programs, or even birthday, anniversary, or other special occasions.

Who doesn't like to be recognized? In fact, when I talk with employees, the feedback I have often received throughout my career is that employees are not feeling appreciated or recognized for their efforts.

Depending on your business, you may have a program to recognize your staff for meeting certain sales quotas, receiving compliments from customers or clients, or when certification or other educational goals are achieved.

There are a number of reasons to recognize your employees and communicating that information at the beginning of one's employment is a way to show your new employee how much they are appreciated.

66. Career development/advancement opportunities

If your experience in interviewing is anything like mine, you probably talk with a lot of candidates where career advancement, or development, is important to them. So why not include information in your orientation about the various opportunities within your company?

This will be particularly good if you are a larger company where, after a certain period of time, employees may be able to apply for other opportunities. If there are specific steps towards advancing within your company, communicate that in your orientation too.

If there are opportunities for certification programs, tuition reimbursement, or specialized training at your company that would also assist in one's career development, that information could be included as well.

Invite someone to specifically talk about the career development paths and/or advancement opportunities during your orientation meeting. This will offer an excellent opportunity for your new employee to ask any questions they may have at that time.

67. Special group or committee

I remember working for a company where I led an active and creative employee relations committee.

We pulled off some pretty amazing events such as a bowling competition that was huge success, and a very elegant Christmas party event in the office.

Perhaps you have a special group or committee that could participate in your orientation meeting? Do you have a Safety Committee or a committee that writes all of the birthday cards for each employee's birthday?

If so, they can share this during orientation and offer any new employee the opportunity to join that committee.

By providing opportunities for your new employee to work with a team, it will increase their sense of belonging right away.

Provide information on a flyer or handout as part of a PowerPoint presentation, or have an invited guest from that committee present at your orientation meeting.

68. Independent assignments

Ultimately, you will want your newly hired employee to be able to work independently in certain parts of their job. Here are a couple of ideas you could consider:

Individual Checklist –Give your new employee a checklist of items that should be completed within a set timeframe (i.e., 1 week). The items on this checklist could include tasks such as: locate the employee bulletin board, time clock, and completing certain forms or processes.

Individual Interviews –Provide a list of key individuals to interview. You could also include a list of suggested questions as well.

69. Special Fund

A fund could be established where employees can contribute a couple of dollars each month for cards, gifts, and cakes for new employees, as well as for other employee events.

Above and Beyond

One of the things Human Resource professionals find challenging about their new employee orientation program is thinking of ideas that go above and beyond the basics.

The following 10 ideas do just that. These are suggestions that are certainly not required for your program, but with a little creativity, could yield that wow factor you may be seeking for your program:

70. Red carpet

How cool would it be to add a real red carpet to the orientation process? It could be rolled out at a staff meeting, or on their first day. You can have all of the staff standing around the carpet while the new employee walks down (or is escorted down) the red carpet with cheers and whistles from the team welcoming them to the company. This will certainly make them feel like a star for the day! You could have pictures taken for the newsletter, etc.

I'll have to admit that there is a something about a

red carpet that gets people excited. I recall being at a conference for a club I belonged to, and part of the meeting always involved any member, who had attained a certain level of achievement, was eligible to walk down the red carpet for all to see.

If you don't want t use a real red carpet, you can consider having a photo station with a background with a red carpet for new hires to pose for a new hire photo for fun.

71. New hire welcome banner

Now some of you may think this a bit dramatic but honestly, I have seen banners used for many occasions - so why not as part of new hire orientation? Keep the message very general like, "Welcome to company name" and then it can be used multiple times for many occasions.

I've seen banners used to welcome new employees from an acquisition, for safety programs, and recognition weeks. It could be hung in an entrance to welcome your new employee, in the meeting room, or any area where an employee lunch, reception, or meeting will be held.

72. Pep rally

A great way to welcome your new employee is with a pep rally. It could include music, food, and the entire staff to meet your new hire. This is especially effective if you have multiple new hires. It offers an opportunity to get employees excited, and to show your new hires your organization is a fun place to work.

Now this idea came to me when I worked for a company where we acquired many new employees: we provided them t-shirts, food, and music, along with their new hire packets. Speakers and employees who worked at nearby locations came and spoke about their experience with the company.

It was such a positive and fun experience that it stuck out as something that could be done at any time there is was new group of employees joining the company.

73. New hire get together

Here is an idea where you can plan for all of your newly hired employees to get together for lunch, a pizza party, dinner, or other activity that would be appropriate for your company. This allows the new employee's time to chat in a casual atmosphere where they can discuss things other than the new job.

To encourage conversation, distribute pieces of paper with a question already printed on it. These questions could be of a variety of things such as; where they were born, favorite foods or hobbies.

By including current employees, you are encouraging an interaction where your new employee may also share their feelings about the company, their transition, etc. This is all important information to gauge if your process is effective or not.

74. Balloons

You can never go wrong with displaying balloons to celebrate your new hire's arrival. Whether a small amount to put on a table where they will be doing paperwork, or a huge display to place in any area where all employees and visitors can see, they are an excellent way to bring life into any room or area.

If you are holding your orientation in a conference room, auditorium, or classroom, it will certainly add a little excitement in the room. Balloons, along with any other decorative ideas, could be considered.

75. Projects

Within the first few weeks of employment, schedule a project for new hires along with current employees. This can be a work-related project, or you could choose a volunteer project that is completed outside of the office.

Focusing on a project as a team will give each member insight about their fellow co-workers. It also is an opportunity for managers to observe the role each employee takes on as a part of a team, such as those who are good at problem-solving, or others who exhibit leadership abilities.

76. New employee fair

Here is an idea where you can have all employee services and benefits in a room together at different stations where your new hires can get additional information from each group. Include vendors that work with your organization such as your benefit providers, cell phone company, or office supply companies that offer employee discount programs.

Have departments there to discuss information such as your office management person, someone from IT, or finance, to discuss reports, systems, etc.

How about a station for health and wellness activities such as blood pressure screenings? These activities come handy in making your employee understand and gain more respect for the company.

77. Video presentation featuring your new hire

What better way for your new hire to feel like a star then by having them star in their own video? Here is an idea where you could have a camera or webcam set-up where you do a brief interview with your new hire.

Once completed, it can be shown during an all staff meeting, in the break room, during an online meeting, or training, or wherever it would be appropriate.

You could even include it as part of your orientation presentation where you use the interview as a brief commercial break throughout the day in between sections. That way each new hire is highlighted.

78. Video presentation featuring the team

Similar to the video idea for your new hires, have current employees produce a video to share with your new hire.

Include several team members saying hello and welcoming your new hire (by name, if possible). Or it could have a welcome message by department.

79. Employee testimonials

Select a handful of current employees to write something about a day in the life of working for your company. Have them include their picture, department, position title, and length of service. Have them write a few paragraphs about a recent event, what it's like to be in a certain position or anything that would help your new employee get a feel for what it's like to work at your company.

This could also be in a video format and included in your orientation presentation or online.

Final Thoughts

You have now had a chance to review 79 ideas for your orientation program. I am hopeful that there are a few ideas or suggestion included that will assist you in taking your orientation program to the next level.

I recognize that the recruitment process is a huge effort, so losing new employees because they don't feel welcome or part of the team is in most cases a preventable occurrence. As human resource professionals, we want to assist in the retention of employees, so this is a good way to achieve that goal by getting them started off in the right foot.

The following 11 ideas are some final things to think about when it comes to your program, your new employees, and activities that should continue well after their initial orientation meeting.

If I could sum up my thoughts on why employees may feel left to fend for themselves in a new work environment, I would describe this in the follow 3 points:

1. Poor follow-up after the orientation meeting;
2. Lack of, or poor communication; and
3. No clear expectations set.

Here are some ideas that will address these barriers to having highly motivated employees throughout their first few months of employment.

80. Training plan

As part of your orientation program, you will want to ensure that there is a full training plan in place. One that includes the basic information needed for them to learn their job and about the company.

In addition to any training that HR is conducting, you will want to ensure that the specific department they will be working in has a training plan as well. By partnering with your department managers, you will become more knowledgeable of what is required for each department.

Upon your review, you can make suggestions or

recommendations to ensure that the training is at an appropriate pace so that employees are not feeling overwhelmed. It is also good way for you to be reassured that there is an actual plan in place, and is being followed.

Using a checklist or spreadsheet has worked very well for me with the follow-up on a training plan. Include the name and description of training (from all areas, not just HR), the date the training occurred, and any training notes for each item. When training is completed, you will have a document that shows all the training that has been completed, by whom, when, etc.

This could be posted as a shared document and accessible by all who participate in the training process. That way they can update their respective training areas with notes and date(s) of the training.

81. Early performance evaluation

Performance evaluation should be a continuous process, so providing early feedback is another way to reassure your new employee that they are meeting expectations and starting off on the right track.

If there are opportunities for improvement, even at the early stages of employment, then communicating that with gentle coaching may be all that is needed to turn things around.

There could be a quick performance review after the first week, then again at 30 days, then 90 days. Thereafter, it could be incorporated into your regular performance review process going forward. This allows the manager to provide feedback, as well as the new employee to provide feedback, early on. If there are any concerns or questions from the new hire, they can be discussed and addressed right away.

A process like this will let your new employee know that their opinion matters and they have support to assist them in being successful.

82. Post-orientation interview

Within the first few months of employment, another idea you could implement as the HR person is to schedule a post-orientation interview with new hires. Ask them questions about their transition, what is working, what are some areas of opportunity, and is there anything that you can assist them with.

There may be some things they are experiencing that they may feel more comfortable sharing with you as the HR person. Whether good or bad, you can certainly act on the feedback and help facilitate a timely resolution.

83. Be caring

It is easy to forget what it is like to be new at a company. As a result, there can be a lack of empathy of what that new employee may be going through.

This is particularly true if they are not only new to your company, but perhaps they are new to the area because they relocated, or just returning to the workforce after not working for a period of time.

Whatever the case may be, just showing that you care about them as a person can go a long way.

Just checking in on them to see how things are going, or asking for any suggestions they may have to ensure a smooth transition, is important. Not just on the first day, but within the first several weeks and even beyond.

84. Be professional

One of the worst things that could happen in the new hire process is to have your new employee experience unprofessional conduct by someone at your company.

Under no circumstances should any employee be allowed to behave in an unprofessional manner with your new hire, current employee, customer, clients, etc. While these behaviors can be addressed specifically with the offending employee, unfortunately, the damage is already done with regard to your new employee and the impression of the company they just joined has been tarnished.

I remember a time in one of the companies I worked for where there was an employee disgruntled about being asked to participate in the orientation process. As a result, her desire to be anywhere else, besides participating in an orientation meeting, showed throughout her communication and interactions; and needless to say, she did not represent the company well.

Another point here is to make sure everyone who is participating in the orientation process is clear about the expectations of being friendly, welcoming, and professional.

85. Communication

I have already listed a few ideas that will assist with communication such as early performance discussions and post-orientation interviews. Other methods of communication are memos, emails, newsletters, staff meetings, etc.

If you have any gaps in communication, be proactive and fill them right away. Communication should not just occur on the first day, but should be continuous throughout the remainder of their employment with your company.

The other point I want to reiterate about communication, is to also ensure the communication is professional, positive, and respectful.

A lot of issues I deal with from an employee relations perspective often deal with how someone communicated with them; how they felt they were not talked to with respect; or there was not enough communication at all.

86. Teamwork

The more that your new employee feels a part of the team, the better chance you will have in retaining that person. Unfortunately, in some work environments, there are many cliques in the workplace. This can make it quite difficult for someone new to feel accepted as part of the team.

If you know these dynamics exist in certain departments, or at any level, offer to work with that department manager to address it prior to the new hire's arrival. Furthermore, encourage that manager to create as many opportunities to promote teamwork as possible.

This could include encouraging the existing team to assist with part of your new employee's training. Select a current employee to do some one-on-one training, or even assign them to work on a task together.

87. Meetings

After the orientation meeting, hopefully there will be ongoing meetings occurring that will assist the new employee in keeping up with important information within the department, and the company as whole.

There should be regular department staff meetings, (generally weekly or every other week), as well as a monthly all employee meetings with all of the staff at your location.

Having regular meetings is one way for new employees, (and all employees), to count on that information will be provided on things that are important to them in a timely manner.

88. Peaceful & positive work environment

I cannot stress enough that ensuring that the work environment is as peaceful and positive as possible can make for very happy employees. Nobody wants to work in an environment where there is constant arguing, bad attitudes, and disrespectful conduct.

If this is occurring in your workplace, it needs to be addressed immediately, and hopefully before your new hire arrives. There are many constructive ways to work through conflicts, so employees need to understand the options and not infect the morale of the entire team or department.

89. Frequently asked questions

Having a handout available with your most frequently asked questions is a great tool to have. Include questions and answers to things like, "When do I get my first paycheck?" or "When do I sign up for benefits?"

This can be provided at any time during the process, such as with the offer letter, on the first day, or any time afterwards.

90. Suggestions

My final idea is to think about a suggestion box or other ways to get suggestions on improving your orientation process. We have discussed a survey, early performance review, and post–orientation interviews, to get some information.

In an effort to cover all bases, and capture those who have something to say, but for whatever reason feel more comfortable sharing feedback anonymously this is another great tool to help determine the effectiveness of your program.

There you have it, 90 suggestions and ideas to assist with moving your new employee orientation program forward to the next level. Again, several ideas that are broken into several categories that will help you organize which ideas you what to work on now, and which ideas you would like to incorporate at a later time.

30 Bonus New Employee Orientation Ideas

As a bonus, I would like to share with you 30 additional new employee orientation ideas that can bring new energy into your process.

Throughout this guide there has been a lot of discussion about how the orientation process is such a critical component of your new employee's introduction to the company. It is also a way to demonstrate a company that is committed to achieving its business goals, as well as having a little fun along the way.

Therefore, in no particular order, the following are 30 additional ideas you can consider incorporating into your process as appropriate.

1. Create an app- Have a special app developed just for new hires. Inside the app can include a variety of helpful information. This could include access to company videos, parking information, the orientation agenda, frequently asked questions, and more.

2. Personalized products - You could research different companies that customize various products with your new employee's name on it and/or other customized text. This could include bags, t-shirts, cups or any other types of products that you prefer.

3. Life-size poster board photo – Consider having a life-size stand-up poster of a key individual(s) who may be unable to attend the orientation. Your new hire could then take a picture next to it and it can be featured in a fun way such as in a newsletter, or presentation where all employees can see.

4. Photo book – Particularly if there is a large group of new hires, you can have each person submit a photo of themselves electronically in advance to be included in a photo book of all the new hires. Underneath each photo could include a few facts about each new hire.

5. Create a theme – You could have a clever theme for your next orientation that include activities that relate to the theme. The theme could be related to a company culture initiative, mission, or any other areas of focus at the time. You could also use other theme ideas such as a cruise theme and have lots of fun with it. For example, you can create sections in the meeting room and give them a name such as "Handbook Island". That would be a destination new hires go for a presentation on the handbook. In keeping with this sample theme you could also have managers present your new hires with a tropical flavored beverage with an umbrella in it. You can explore other themes as well such as the 80's, 90's, sports or movie themes.

6. **Create break-out sessions** – You can organize the orientation where certain topics are presented in break-out sessions in different rooms or locations. You could break up the group of new employees into smaller groups and together they could rotate into different break-out sessions. This allows for greater variety in meeting location, and the ability for your new hires to get to know each other better in a smaller group.

7. Cake/cupcakes with each new employee's name – You could have a cake (or cupcakes) and list each new employees name on the cake. When it is time to cut the cake, each new hire would get the piece with their name on it. Or if using cupcakes, each would receive the cupcake with their individual name written on it.

8. **New hire talent show** - You could have a portion of the orientation meeting to allow for either the new hire participants and/or current employees to show off their talent. This could be accomplished in between presentations like a "commercial break". Or there could be time dedicated in the orientation program for it to occur all at once such as during the lunch hour. The talent could be a display of something each participant does well at work and/or could be other forms of talent as appropriate.

9. **Yearbook** – With this idea, you could have pictures taken throughout the entire orientation program. After the orientation has ended, all the pictures can be put together in a yearbook format and presented to each new hire of their orientation experience. You can also have employees in their department to sign it before presenting. You can also lay out the yearbook in areas where candidates would be located; or bring them to career fairs as another recruitment tool.

10. Live entertainment - Who does not like live entertainment? You can hire a pianist or any other type of musician to come in and play background music at the very beginning of the orientation meeting where meet and greet activities would be occurring. You can also have them play during the lunch hour and/or in between breaks.

11. Retention roundtable/panel – Another idea to consider is an employee retention roundtable or panel to discuss retention ideas your new hires may have. Here they can share their expectations and experiences that may help capture additional retention ideas for future new hires and existing staff.

12. Motivational speaker – To energize the group of new employees before starting in their new roles, you can have a motivational speaker that presents to the group. There focus can be on a variety of topics such as success stories of others who have joined the company, how to accomplish goals; or to motivate them about the great company they will be working for.

13. Relaxation techniques – There is generally some level of stress in most positions, some more than others. Therefore, a portion of the orientation could include a focus on relaxation techniques and stress-management in the workplace.

14. Gifts for family members - You could set up a table with different items where your new hires can pick and choose items for their family members. Or you can create a form with various items for them to select for their family members. A gift bag with the selected items would then be given to them at the end of the orientation to take and present to their families on behalf of their new company.

15. Pets on parade – For those new hires who are interested, you could have them send in an electronic picture of their beloved pet and include in the presentations throughout the orientation. Each slide could be the picture of the pet, the pet's name and the name of the new employee they belong to. Imagine how welcomed your new employee will feel when they see their beloved pet on the screen as part of the orientation presentation.

16. Virtual vacation – Here you can consider another idea in between orientation presentations. You can show videos, pictures, or brochures of different vacation destination and have them just think about that vacation spot briefly. You can include music from that destination as well to add to the experience. So for example you can say during the break, "Now we are headed to Maui" – then play island music or a quick video you can find online that can be played for just a few minutes.

17. Orientation judges – You can have the new hires judge each section after each presenter has finished. You could provide several ballots at the beginning and ask participants to score the presentation and provide comments. You could ask a new employee to be the volunteer to collect the ballots after each presentation and place them in the designated location. While a survey at the end of the orientation is still a good method for getting feedback about the orientation program, this approach allows you to get their feedback sooner while the experience is still fresh in their mind.

18. Speed meetings – You could have a portion of the orientation where employees get to sit and talk with key leaders, management and other current employees in a large room one-on-one. These would be quick one-on-one meetings where they get approximately 5 or 10 minutes with each individual. Then at the end of the allotted time, they switch to talk with another individual. This could continue for about 4 - 6 rounds. This would be another opportunity for your new hires to get to know other employees in the company quicker.

19. Themed gift baskets – You could create themed gift baskets that can be raffled off during each section of the orientation. For example, if the topic of safety is being presented, there could be a safety basket that would be raffled off or given to the individual who can answer a safety question correctly. The gift basket could include all sorts of safety related items that they can use at work or at home. This could be expanded to several other topics and themes as well.

20. Individual tour guide - In addition to any group tour you may have, you can have an additional portion of the orientation where each new hire is assigned an individual tour guide. This will allow your new employee to spend time with a current employee who can go into more detail of certain areas that may be more department specific. It is a more personal approach to helping your new hire become familiar with the workplace.

21. Orientation fun bucks – With this idea, you can establish a process where your new employees can have an opportunity to earn fun bucks or tickets throughout the orientation. This could be accomplished by answering certain questions, or any other approach you would like. At the end of the orientation, they can use their fun bucks or tickets to purchase certain items such as treats, company merchandise or any other items that may be available.

22. A day in the life of a new hire - You can coordinate a documentary style video of a new hire that can be shown during the orientation program. Here you would interview a new employee during the first few months of employment and capture it all on video. You can add footage with follow-up interviews each quarter for up to a year. The interviews would include feedback and advice for other new hires about their experience. By showing this during new employee orientation, it gives participants a better idea of what to expect.

23. Company cheer team – You can have a group of current employees volunteer to participant in the orientation program by performing a welcome cheer. This could be the kick-off for the orientation where employees dressed in company gear (and pom-poms if desired) come out and actually perform a cheer with chants that express a welcome and excitement that have joined the company.

24. Team building ideas – There are various ways to help a group of new employees get to know each other better during the orientation meeting(s). While participants in the orientation may or may not work together in the same role, departments or locations; in most cases, they are still a part of the same company. So finding ways for participants to have an engaging experience with each other as a group can create a greater sense of feeling a part of team and building relationships right away. To achieve this, there are several teambuilding activities you can incorporate into the orientation. This could include an expansion on the games ideas; or include an actual group exercise where they would have to work in teams such as a sports activity, task or group presentation.

25. Ongoing welcome communication- You can have a series of follow-up communication to your new hires that start after the initial new employee orientation program has ended. This could be specific reminders about certain items that were covered during orientation such as: parking details; reminders on who to contact for various items; or meal suggestions for the lunch hour as appropriate. This communication could also include quick videos, checklists, additional FAQ's and more.

26. Role playing - - You can have participants and/or current employees participate in role playing activities to further re-inforce orientation content. This could include such topics as customer service, professional vs unprofessional conduct; or examples of how to deal with conflict. Another role-playing exercise could include an actual skit that could be presented in a variety of ways. For example, you could break the group up into teams and have them each create a skit on a particular relevant topic and perform it in front of the group; or you can have a skit prepared in advance to be presented by current staff.

27. Additional transportation ideas – Where it makes sense you can offer a special valet parking service for your new hires attending the orientation meeting; particularly if parking is limited; or far away. You can also consider arranging special transportation where you could pick up your new employee from a designated location such as their home, hotel, or a certain location on-site. They could be picked up in a limo, a town car, or company vehicle as appropriate.

28. **Welcome gift to the home** – With this idea you can consider sending each newly hired employee a welcome gift directly to the home. This could include a flower bouquet, fruit basket, fancy coffee/tea basket or something similar with a nice welcome message.

29. Employee fashion show – To add a nice variety to your orientation program, you can present a fashion show that shows both the appropriate and inappropriate ways to dress for work. This could be a live fashion show or a video presentation of a prior fashion show.

30. Awards presentation - To end your initial new employee orientation program, you can present a certificate or small trophy to each participant for their participation. You could create categories such as "most questions asked" or "first person to arrive" where a new hire would receive the award for that category.

You now have 120 new employee orientation ideas that I hope will be helpful in thinking about ways to enhance your own program. I am so excited about all the potential that exists in taking your new employee orientation program to a new level.

Get Ready – Set – GO!!

I would like to offer my well wishes to you as you go back and look at your new employee orientation in a new light. I also hope this information has motivated you to make your orientation program the type of program you know it can be.

Now for some of you, making changes to your new employee orientation program will be relatively easy. You may be in a situation where you can pretty much move forward with implementing ideas and suggestions with good support. If this is your situation, then I am very excited about the next steps you plan on taking with your new employee orientation and would love to hear about your progress.

For others, I completely understand that you may have a few steps you may have to take. In fact, you may be thinking to yourself that you have all of these great ideas now, but you are not sure if others in your company or department will see the value of putting the time, money, and/or resources towards enhancing this process.

For those of you in that situation, I want to encourage you with a few suggestions to assist you in getting support on the changes you may want to recommend:

1. **Turnover data** - Be prepared with any sort of turnover data that you can share. Particularly if you are experiencing high turnover, you can present some of the ideas you have to enhance your orientation program as a solution that could impact employee retention.

One area to focus on can be the number of new hires, and how many have left within 3-6 months from hire. If there is a significant high number in this area, then introduce a solution to address with the new employee orientation ideas you think would be most effective in addressing that issue.

2. **Feedback** – Use one of the methods discussed to obtain feedback from recent new hires. If there are areas of opportunities that were expressed in the feedback, then again, this is another opportunity to propose a solution – which would be your recommendations to enhance the program.

3. **One step at a time** – There are a lot of suggestions here, but there is no reason you couldn't take it one step at a time and start with small, low-cost or no-cost suggestions, then over time work your way up to some of the bigger suggestions.

6-Step Plan

I have shared a lot of ideas and suggestions to assist you with your new employee orientation program. As promised, I will now recap these ideas for you in an easy 6-step plan. I have organized all 90 suggestions and ideas into a checklist format. The following is a step-by- step process to follow to get you started.

Note: This checklist is available as a free download at:
http://hrinventurenetwork.com/orientation-checklist/

1. First, go down the checklist and simply mark the items that you feel you have already completed, or ideas that are already included in your program.

2. Next, go through the list again and highlight in yellow the items you feel need to be incorporated into your program right away.

3. Now go through the list for a third time and cross out the items that just do not apply to your company.

4. Finally, go through the list one last time and highlight, in any other color, the items you may want to consider for the future.

5. Now you have a working list of the next steps to create or enhance your new hire orientation program. Review your working list and select your top 3 items, (in yellow) that you would like to incorporate into your program. Once completed, start on your next three, and so on, until all the yellow items have been incorporated.

6. Once all the items in yellow are completed, then start working on the second group of items that were highlighted in a different color. Select your top 1-2 items at a time.

New Employee Orientation Review & Checklist

Step 1: Getting Started

- ☐ 1. Review and compile all the information on your existing program
- ☐ 2. Listen and act on feedback on current process
- ☐ 3. Consider a work group or committee
- ☐ 4. Have a planning meeting with all those who participate in the orientation process
- ☐ 5. Traditional and/or web based program
- ☐ 6. New hire website
- ☐ 7. Pre-boarding/onboarding process
- ☐ 8. Orientation meeting locations
- ☐ 9. Orientation budget

Step 2: The Basics

- ☐ 10. A welcome message
- ☐ 11. A welcome phone call
- ☐ 12. Prepare for your new hire
- ☐ 13. Computer access, emails accounts, and passwords
- ☐ 14. Laptop, cell phones, etc.
- ☐ 15. Business cards and office equipment

- [ ] 16. Badges, name tags, uniforms
- [ ] 17. Introduction to the team
- [ ] 18. New hire lunch
- [ ] 19. Tour
- [ ] 20. Telephone procedures
- [ ] 21. Security/security codes
- [ ] 22. Orientation presentation
- [ ] 23. Orientation speakers
- [ ] 24. Company mission, culture and values
- [ ] 25. Workplace videos
- [ ] 26. Paperwork & new hire packet
- [ ] 27. Employee handbook review
- [ ] 28. Job description review
- [ ] 29. Policies and procedures
- [ ] 30. Payroll
- [ ] 31. Business hours
- [ ] 32. Dress code
- [ ] 33. Organizational chart
- [ ] 34. Benefits and health & wellness
- [ ] 35. State and industry specific requirements
- [ ] 36. Workplace safety

Step 3: Additional Ideas that Rock

- [ ] 37. Personal profile

- ☐ 38. Welcome letter from President
- ☐ 39. Welcome gift/gift basket
- ☐ 40. Post picture of new hire
- ☐ 41. Welcome stand near entrance
- ☐ 42. Newsletter
- ☐ 43. New hire buddy/mentor
- ☐ 44. Games
- ☐ 45. Raffle
- ☐ 46. Scavenger hunt
- ☐ 47. New employee reception
- ☐ 48. Brown bag lunch with all new hires
- ☐ 49. Complimentary meal
- ☐ 50. All employee meeting recognition
- ☐ 51. Welcome book/picture
- ☐ 52. List/brochure of nearby locations
- ☐ 53. Transportation information
- ☐ 54. Parking spot
- ☐ 55. Health & wellness activities
- ☐ 56. Benefit orientation for family members
- ☐ 57. Perks and discounts
- ☐ 58. Department rotation
- ☐ 59. Links to tools and resources
- ☐ 60. Donate for a cause
- ☐ 61. Volunteer opportunities

- ☐ 62. Company activities
- ☐ 63. Complimentary uniform, tools, materials
- ☐ 64. Company merchandise
- ☐ 65. Employee recognition opportunities
- ☐ 66. Career development/advancement opportunities
- ☐ 67. Special group or committee
- ☐ 68. Independent assignment
- ☐ 69. Special fund

Step 4: Even more ideas Above and Beyond

- ☐ 70. Red carpet
- ☐ 71. Welcome banner
- ☐ 72. Pep rally
- ☐ 73. New hire get together
- ☐ 74. Balloons
- ☐ 75. Projects
- ☐ 76. New employee fair
- ☐ 77. Video presentation (new hire)
- ☐ 78. Video presentation (team)
- ☐ 79. Testimonials

Step 5: Final Thoughts

- ☐ 80. Training plan

- ❐ 81. Early performance evaluation
- ❐ 82. Post-orientation interview
- ❐ 83. Be caring
- ❐ 84. Be professional
- ❐ 85. Communication
- ❐ 86. Teamwork
- ❐ 87. Meetings
- ❐ 88. Peaceful & positive work environment
- ❐ 89. Frequently asked questions
- ❐ 90. Suggestions

Bonus Ideas

- ❐ 1. Create an app
- ❐ 2. Personalized products
- ❐ 3. Life-size poster board photo –
- ❐ 4. Photo book
- ❐ 5. Create a theme
- ❐ 6. Create break-out sessions
- ❐ 7. A cake/cupcakes with all new employees' names
- ❐ 8. New hire talent show
- ❐ 9. New employee orientation yearbook
- ❐ 10. Live entertainment
- ❐ 11. Retention roundtable/panel
- ❐ 12. Motivational speaker.

- [ ] 13. Relaxation techniques
- [ ] 14. Gifts for family members
- [ ] 15. Pets on parade
- [ ] 16. Virtual vacation
- [ ] 17. Orientation judges
- [ ] 18. Speed meetings
- [ ] 19. Themed gift baskets
- [ ] 20. Individual tour guide
- [ ] 21. Orientation fun bucks
- [ ] 23. Company cheer team
- [ ] 24. Team building ideas
- [ ] 25. Ongoing welcome communication
- [ ] 26. Role playing
- [ ] 27. Additional transportation ideas
- [ ] 28. Welcome gift to the home.
- [ ] 29. Employee fashion show
- [ ] 30. Awards presentation

Congratulations! By completing these 6 steps, you are on your way to providing a thorough orientation program for your new employees. Furthermore, as an HR professional, you are providing another example of how what you do for your employees, department, and the company every day adds tremendous value as an HR partner within your organization.

Unfortunately, many times we go through training programs or read various articles or books and discover some really good ideas. However, as soon as we return to our regular routine, we forget all about them, or simply choose not to take action.

I want to encourage you not to let that happen to your new employee orientation program. Take another look at your working checklist and assign yourself realistic due dates for the steps needed to complete this process for your program. Mark these dates in your calendar, with reminders to assist you with keeping you on track each step of the way.

Finally, don't let this important task get away from you. This resource was created with you in mind, so please feel free to use these ideas and customize them to fit your situation and your orientation program goals.

Remember, as a professional in HR, enhancing your new employee orientation program is not only good for new hires and the company; it's also a great way to re-energize your own HR career. This is an opportunity to lead a project, share your ideas; and work with others to create a program that can positively impact employee retention, engagement and overall satisfaction. That's exciting!! In fact, the possibilities are endless on what you can create when you think of all of the ideas you can try for your new employee orientation process.

So here's to your success with your new employee orientation program and in igniting your own HR career.

http://hrinventurenetwork.com

Email: Alisa@hrinventurenetwork.com

If you liked this guide, then you may be interested in the following journals for HR professionals also by

Alisa Charles

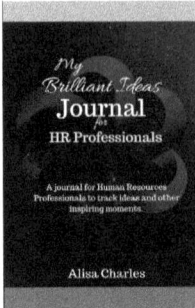

My Brilliant Ideas Journal
for HR Professionals

A journal for Human Resources Professionals to track ideas and other inspiring moments.

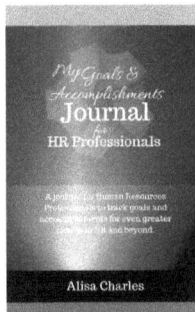

My Goals & Accomplishments Journal for HR Professionals

A journal for Human Resources Professionals to track goals and accomplishments for even greater results in HR and beyond.

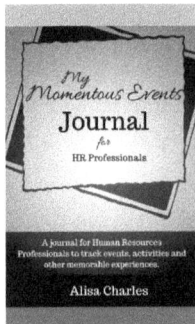

My Momentous Events Journal
for HR Professionals

A journal for Human Resources Professionals to track events, activities and other impactful experiences.

Also a great gift idea for your favorite HR person or team

All available at
www.hrinventurenetwork.com/journals4HR
www.hrinventurenetwork.com/coolmugs4HR